To... Shirley

From... Wanda and Rich

Aug. 2002.

For my nephew, Jason, with love

Text copyright © 2000
Peter Pauper Press, Inc.
202 Mamaroneck Avenue
White Plains, NY 10601
All rights reserved
ISBN 0-88088-116-X
Printed in China
9 8 7

Visit us at www.peterpauper.com

A Beacon
of Light

✕✕✕

Paths to Wisdom

There are two ways of spreading light:
to be the candle or the mirror
that reflects it.

Edith Wharton

Hope is the feeling you have
that the feeling you have
isn't permanent.

Jean Kerr

Be not afraid of growing slowly, be
afraid only of standing still.

Chinese Proverb

Remember this: Now is the only
time you have. . . . Later doesn't exist.
Creation doesn't know anything but
now. Whenever you get around to doing
what you want to do, it will be now.

Bernie S. Siegel, M.D.

There are only two ways to live your life. One is as though nothing is a miracle, the other is as though everything is a miracle.

Albert Einstein

Always be a first-rate version of yourself, instead of a second-rate version of somebody else.

Judy Garland

I avoid looking forward or
backward, and try to keep
looking upward.

Charlotte Brontë

When you get to the end
of your rope, tie a knot
and hang on.

Anonymous

The block of granite which is an
obstacle in the pathway of the weak,
becomes a stepping stone in the
pathway of the strong.

Thomas Carlyle

Rather than a soul in a body,
become a body in a soul.
Reach for your soul.
Reach even farther.

Gary Zukav

The purpose of this life and
all of its experiences is not
to make ourselves what we
think we should be. It is to
unfold as what we already are.
We are already powerful,
divine, wise, loving beings.

Iyanla Vanzant

What we sow is what we reap.
And when we choose actions that
bring happiness and success to
others, the fruit of our karma
is happiness and success.

Deepak Chopra

If you won't be you, who will?
If not now, when?

Lee Ezell

Strange as it may seem, life becomes
serene and enjoyable precisely when
selfish pleasure and personal success
are no longer the guiding goals.

Mihaly Csikszentmihalyi

Common people are brilliant if only
they believe in their own ideas.

Robert H. Schuller

A smooth sea never made
a skilled mariner.

English Proverb

When in doubt, make a fool of
yourself. There is a microscopically
thin line between being brilliantly
creative and acting like the
most gigantic idiot on earth.
So what the hell, leap.

Cynthia Heimel

As long as I continue to stay
in the present, I am happy
forever: because forever is
always the present.

Spencer Johnson

Follow your bliss.

Joseph Campbell

Buddha left a road map,
Jesus left a road map, Krishna left a
road map, Rand McNally left a
road map. But you still have to
travel the road yourself.

Stephen Levine

The sound body is the product
of the sound mind.

George Bernard Shaw

When you make a world tolerable
for yourself, you make a world
tolerable for others.

Anaïs Nin

We often look elsewhere for
what we have already; we project.
We turn to others to give us
a level of acceptance we can
only give ourselves.

Jill Mellick

©WEGNER

Freedom is not the goal;
but you need freedom before you
can decide what the goal is!

Ashleigh Brilliant

———⦙⦙⦙———

When I find my focus and keep
my balance—I find that all is
right with my world.

Thomas Kinkade

What you do is vaguely interesting,
who you are is inspiring.

Rita Hogarth

Look well into thyself; there
is a source of strength which
will always spring up if thou
wilt always look there.

Marcus Aurelius

Be brave enough to live life creatively. The creative is the place where no one else has ever been. You have to leave the city of your comfort and go into the wilderness of your intuition. You can't get there by bus, only by hard work and risk and by not quite knowing what you're doing. What you'll discover will be wonderful. What you'll discover will be yourself.

Alan Alda,
to his daughter

We could never learn to be
brave and patient, if there were
only joy in the world.

Helen Keller

We don't know who we are until
we see what we can do.

Martha Grimes

Experience is not what happens
to you; it is what you do with
what happens to you.

Aldous Huxley

If you do not believe in yourself,
do not blame others for
lacking faith in you.

Brendan Francis

What lies behind us and what
lies before us are tiny matters
compared to what lies within us.

Ralph Waldo Emerson

To be a great champion you
must believe you are the best.
If you're not, pretend you are.

Muhammad Ali

Let every man's hope be in himself.

Virgil

To hope is to believe in humanity;
and in its future. Hope remains the
highest reality, the age-old power;
hope is at the root of all the great ideas
and causes that have bettered the lot
of humankind across the centuries.

Ronald Reagan

A woman is like a teabag.
You don't know her strength
until she is in hot water.

Nancy Reagan

When you feel depressed
and out of sorts, pause and
read the comics.

Brian Adams

Hope is the thing with feathers,
That perches in the soul,
And sings the tune
without the words,
And never stops at all.

Emily Dickinson

Too much of a good thing
is wonderful.

Mae West

If you are what you do,
when you don't you aren't.

William J. Byron, S.J.

We try to grasp too much
of life at a time. We think of
it as a whole, instead of taking the
days one by one. Life is a
mosaic, and each tiny piece
must be cut and set with skill.

Anonymous

It takes an uncommon amount
of guts to put your dreams on the
line, to hold them up and say,
"How good or how bad am I?"
That's where courage comes in.

Erma Bombeck

Your past is important,
but it is not important enough
to control your future.

Zig Ziglar

The cards you hold in the game of
life mean very little—it's the way
you play them that counts.

If we don't change, we don't grow.
If we don't grow, we are not
really living. Growth demands a
temporary surrender of security.

Gail Sheehy

Nothing great was ever achieved
without enthusiasm.

Ralph Waldo Emerson

Spirituality is being awake.
Getting rid of illusions. Spirituality
is never being at the mercy of
any event, thing, or person.
Spirituality means having found
the diamond mine inside yourself.

Anthony DeMello

Again and again we adults
have made a habit of stumbling
upon joy, a different kind from the
one children have but nonetheless
a version that leaves no doubt:
Life is, indeed, a wondrous gift.

Anne Roiphe

Fill what's empty. Empty what's full.

Alice Roosevelt Longworth

You will become as great as your
dominant aspiration. . . . If you
cherish a vision, a lofty ideal in
your heart, you will realize it.

James Allen

If only we'd stop trying to
be happy, we could have
a pretty good time.

Edith Wharton

Much of what we see depends
on what we are looking for.

Phil Calloway

You cannot discover your
passion if you have lost your
ability to enjoy yourself.

Cecile Andrews

We spend the first half of
our lives looking for success.
The second half, we look for
significance. At the end of the
race, you want to be able to
look in the mirror and say,
"This was a life well lived."

Dave Valle,
major league baseball pitcher

Once human consciousness
has changed, once we have a new
awareness of our place in the scheme
of things, once we have realized
that there is more to life than the
unending chase for material
possessions, and once we focus on the
importance of being rather than
having, we will see a dramatic
transformation all around us.

Satish Kumar

Every season, sit down alone
and think about whether you're
happy or not, and whether you
would make the same decisions
you've made if given the chance
to do it all over again.

Marianne Legato, M.D.

Never give up then, for that is just the
place and time the tide will turn.

Harriet Beecher Stowe

So many women just don't know
how great they really are.
They come to us all vogue outside
and vague on the inside.

Mary Kay Ash

The real voyage of discovery consists
not in finding new landscapes,
but in having new eyes.

Marcel Proust

The rainbows of materialism,
power, status and distractions
do not bring the gold of peace,
love and contentment.

Dorothy Corkille Briggs

What do I mean by loving
ourselves properly? I mean first
of all, desiring to live, accepting
life as a very great gift and a great
good, not because of what it
gives us, but because of what it
enables us to give others.

Thomas Merton

To be centered is to say yes to life.
The center joins past and future,
heaven and earth, the near and the
far, the way out and the way in.
It is a secure place from which to
venture forth and to which
you can always return.

George Leonard

Be friendly all the time,
be creative, be courteous, be fun,
be loving, be sure to play,
be empathic, thankful, grateful ...
and serve your butt off!

Patch Adams, M.D.,
volunteer clown

There are times when you all try
to take in so much information that
sometimes you feel overloaded.
Rest in the knowledge that one
person is not required to follow all
paths; one person is not required
to gain all knowledge.

Pauline Larson

Though no one can go back and make a
new start, anyone can start from now,
and make a brand new ending.

Carl Bard

It's good to have an end to
journey toward; but it's the journey
that matters, in the end.

Ursula K. LeGuin

And the day came when the
risk [it took] to remain tight in the
bud was more painful than the
risk it took to blossom.

Anaïs Nin

I'm a great believer in luck,
and I find the harder I work
the more I have of it.

Thomas Jefferson

As you walk and eat and travel,
be where you are. Otherwise you
will miss most of your life.

Buddha

The ocean couldn't be crossed
but Columbus did it.
The Atlantic couldn't be crossed
solo by air, but Lindbergh did it.
The moon was out of reach,
but men have landed on it.

Paul S. McElroy

The new frontier is internal.

John Renesch

If at first you do succeed,
try something harder.

Ann Landers

When you fall, pick up something
while you're down there.

Sherry Conway Appel

There isn't a person anywhere who
isn't capable of doing more
than he thinks he can.

Henry Ford

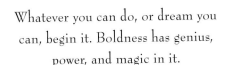

Whatever you can do, or dream you
can, begin it. Boldness has genius,
power, and magic in it.

Goethe

©WEGNER

To get it right, be born with luck or else make it. *Never* give up. Get the knack of getting people to help you and also pitch in yourself. A little money helps, but what *really* gets it right is to *never*—I repeat—*never*, under any condition face the facts.

Ruth Gordon

Believe in yourself!
Have faith in your abilities!
Without a humble but reasonable
confidence in your own powers you
cannot be successful or happy.

Norman Vincent Peale

There is only one success—
to be able to spend your life
in your own way.

Christopher Morley

Be bold—and mighty forces
will come to your aid.

Basil King

Do what you can, with what
you have, where you are.

Theodore Roosevelt

One who overcomes
others has force;
One who overcomes
himself is strong.

Taoist poem

Happiness is as a butterfly,
which, when pursued, is always
beyond our grasp, but which,
if you will sit down quietly,
may alight upon you.

Nathaniel Hawthorne

Hope is like the sun, which,
as we journey toward it,
casts the shadow of our
burden behind us.

Samuel Smiles

To live a good life requires
what is called grace, that is, the
doing for another kindnesses he
doesn't deserve, hasn't earned,
could not ask for, and can't repay.
Grace offers to a person what
he cannot do for himself.

Paul S. McElroy

Faith, like light, should always be
simple and unbending; while love,
like warmth, should beam forth on
every side, and bend to every
necessity of our brethren.

Martin Luther

Have the courage to act
instead of react.

Earlene Larson

The secret of life is not to do what you
like, but to like what you do.

There is a light that shines
beyond all things on earth, beyond
us all, beyond the heavens,
beyond the highest, the very
highest heavens. This is the
Light that shines in our heart.

Chandogya Upanishad

Life is a pure flame and we live by
an invisible sun within us.

Nobody can give you wiser
advice than yourself.

Work is the path for spiritual
development. The outer world
is a mirror. So much of life is
focused on work; it's the best
place to learn our lessons
and offer our gifts.

Judi Neal

I believe happiness and joy
are the purpose of life.

The Dalai Lama

He who considers too much
will perform little.

Johann Friedrich von Schiller

Plant the seeds of expectation
in your mind; cultivate thoughts
that anticipate achievement.
Believe in yourself as being
capable of overcoming all
obstacles and weaknesses.

Norman Vincent Peale

The greatest results in life are usually attained by simple means and the exercise of ordinary qualities. These may for the most part be summed in these two— commonsense and perseverance.

Feltham

In a dark time, the eye begins to see.

Theodore Roethke

One has to be in the same place
every day, watch the dawn from
the same house, hear the same birds
awake each morning, to realize
how inexhaustibly rich and
different is sameness.

Chuang Tzu

What's going on in the inside
shows on the outside.

Earl Nightingale

If a man thinks only in response
to the stimuli of the outer world,
he remains ego only, an automation;
but when he *originates* thoughts at
the center of consciousness, he
creates his own life in the image
of his desires and dons the
mantle of immortal Self.

U. S. Andersen

The way I see it, if you want
the rainbow, you gotta put
up with the rain.

Dolly Parton

The key to fulfillment,
to a wonderful life, is to do
what's in your heart, and to
put your heart into what you do.
Then you'll succeed. Always.

Marc Allen

When a man can still his senses
I call him illuminated.
Sri Krsna